No Holds Barred Fighting:
The Kicking Bible
Strikes for MMA and the Street

Mark Hatmaker

Photography by Doug Werner

TRACKS

Tracks Publishing
San Diego, California

No Holds Barred Fighting:
The Kicking Bible
Mark Hatmaker

Tracks Publishing
140 Brightwood Avenue
Chula Vista, CA 91910
619-476-7125
tracks@cox.net
www.startupsports.com

Copyright © 2008 by Doug Werner
10 9 8 7 6 5 4 3 2 1

Publisher's Cataloging-in-Publication

Hatmaker, Mark.
    No holds barred fighting : the kicking bible :
strikes for MMA and the street / Mark Hatmaker ;
photography by Doug Werner.
    p. cm.
    Includes index.
    LCCN 2008906895
    ISBN-13: 978-1-884654-31-2
    ISBN-10: 1-884654-31-2

    1. Hand-to-hand fighting–Handbooks, manuals, etc.
2. Mixed martial arts–Handbooks, manuals, etc.
3. Wrestling–Handbooks, manuals, etc.   I. Werner,
Doug, 1950- II. Title. III. Title: Kicking bible.

GV1111.H3375 2008   796.81
                    QBI08-600228

Fighting Books by Mark Hatmaker

No Holds Barred Fighting:
The Ultimate Guide to Submission Wrestling

More No Holds Barred Fighting:
Killer Submissions

No Holds Barred Fighting:
Savage Strikes

No Holds Barred Fighting:
Takedowns

No Holds Barred Fighting:
The Clinch

No Holds Barred Fighting:
The Ultimate Guide to Conditioning

No Holds Barred Fighting:
The Kicking Bible

Boxing Mastery

Books are available through major bookstores
and booksellers on the Internet.

Dedication
To the patience of my family and friends who tolerate my habitual withdrawals so I can work on what are essentially combat cookbooks.

And to all of the new friends and readers I have encountered in the course of preparing these violent little recipe manuals. I hope you find what lies within these pages to your tastes.

Acknowledgements
Phyllis Carter
Jackie Smith
Kylie Hatmaker
Mitch Thomas
Shane Tucker
Kory Hays

Warning label
The fighting arts include contact and can be dangerous. Use proper equipment and train safely. Practice with restraint and respect for your partners. Drill for fun, fitness and to improve skills. Do not fight with the intent to do harm.

Contents

HOW TO USE THE NHBF MANUALS

This book and the others in the *No Holds Barred Fighting (NHBF)* series are meant to be used in an interlocking synergistic manner where the sum value of the manuals is greater than the individual parts. What we are striving to do with each manual is to focus on a specific aspect of the twin sports of NHB and submission wrestling and give thoughtful consideration to the necessary ideas, tactics and strategies pertinent to the facet of focus. We are aware that this piecemeal approach may seem lacking if one consumes only one or two manuals at most, but we are confident that once three or more manuals have been studied, the overall picture or method will begin to reveal itself.

Since the manuals are interlocking, there is no single manual in the series that is meant to be complete in and of itself. For example, although *NHBF: Savage Strikes* is a thorough compendium on NHB/self-defense striking, it is bolstered with a side-by-side study of *Boxing Mastery*. While the book *NHBF: Killer Submissions* introduces the idea of chaining submissions and can be used as a solitary tool, it is much stronger with an understanding of the material that preceded it in *NHBF: The Ultimate Guide to Submission Wrestling*.

And so on and so forth with each manual in this series. Now that I've taken your time to explain the method to my madness, let's empty our teacups and examine the low-kick.

Mark Hatmaker

Kick start

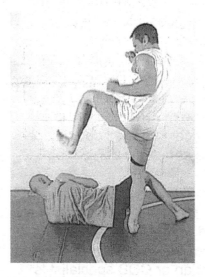

For many, a mention of martial arts conjures mental images of high-flying kicks or spinning kicks launched at impossibly fast cinema speed and devastating MMA knockouts via a bat-cracking, noggin thumping kick to the head. These images often spring foremost because they are the dramatic eye candy fostered by movie choreography and fantastic highlight reels of MMA/NHB matches. For those who yearn to be the next flying kick, spinning top, foot-up-side-the-head sensation, you may want to move on to another book. This one has no drama or eye-catching sensational moves. This book is all about wreaking havoc on your opponent from the belt down.

OK, I've told you what you won't find. Here's what you will find. You will find short, choppy, solid, painful, deceptive (both deceptively painful and painfully deceptive) kicks shot through a prism of pragmatics that will serve all the pertinent needs of the street survivalist, the Close Quarters Battle (CQB) specialist and the MMA/NHB athlete.

When approaching this material it is wise to keep the

author's biases in mind. Because we do not include material on flying kicks, high-kicks and machine gun kicks at high angles does not mean we devalue the athleticism and practice that goes into developing such abilities. On the contrary, such skills are to be admired. Our bias does not state that high-kicks and the ability to kick high are worthless. Rather our bias states that we are odds players, adherents of the Pareto Principle (for more on the Pareto Principle and how it applies to empirical unarmed combat, see our previous volume in this series, *NHBF: Savage Strikes*).

Our bias leans toward the probable — the most likely scenarios in the street and/or MMA competition. Our bias filters the seemingly infinite choices that a mixed martial artist, street technician or CQB specialist is confronted with and pares away material that may be extraneous for our environment. We focus on the finite. This allows us to build greater competency in high percentage tactics rather than be the proverbial jack-of-all-trades, master-of-none. Bruce Lee proffered the same thought in regard to technique paring when he included the following quote from the Tao Te Ching in his own combat-note compilation, *The Tao of Jeet Kune Do*. "It is not daily increase but daily decrease."

Our focus recognizes the scope of material that is, indeed, high percentage must-know material like striking, shooting, grappling and clinch work. There is already more than enough material on those subjects. Diffusing the attention across too many areas causes one to come up with diminishing returns. To become an effective kick specialist as it pertains to the street and MMA, it is not necessary to spin or kick above the belt. Stay with me for a moment. I know a few may immediately grouse and point to the aforementioned highlight reels that feature head-kick knockouts. Yes, these do occur. But before we dismiss the low-kick-only premise out of hand, let's look to a larger sample and see what finishes fights more often than not.

When we examine a large sample of fights where there is no rule that requires a certain number of high-kicks, we see that the majority are won via hands (punches), submissions or simply ground domination. This observation tells us to weight our training odds toward a boxing repertoire, submission work and wrestling control. The head-kick knockout, while dramatic and memorable, is most often anomalous. As for head kicks being the finish in the street, I have yet to see a security tape of a head-kick finish where the opponent wasn't already grounded.

Now, using my own cherry-picking of the data you could point out, "OK, Mark, you say head-kick KOs account for only a fraction of the wins. How many low-kick KOs can you name? None, you say? Yeah, that's what I thought." That point is valid and leads to our next strategic bias. By our way of thinking, kicking is used to punish, to damage and to set up the other high-percentage aspects of the game (hands, subs, ground control). Although we can't point to a significant percentage of wins that occur outright via low-kicks, we can point to quite a few wins that are the direct result of the fighter being punished by low shots. The low shots damaged the opponent and set him up for the high-percentage tools. I think anyone who is even a casual observer of the game can testify to that fact.

Our next bias is one of speed of utility. Humans are precariously balanced on two legs as opposed to the more sure footed four-legged animals. The act of walking is a learned art of balance transfer. Observe toddlers learning to walk or individuals in certain forms of rehab. When both feet remain in contact with the floor, the better the balance — an obvious and perhaps redundant observation, I'm sure. But I can think of no other power intensive sport (and combat sports are indeed power intensive) that actively encourages purposely sacrificing balance for the sake of power. Balance and power are hand-in-glove attributes — sacrifice one and the other declines appreciably.

Don't get me wrong. We know that power with pre-carious balance can be trained and refined to an impressive degree as we see with many of the more talented kicking specialists. But we can also point to quite a few fights where missed (and sometimes not missed) high-kicks result in the kicker slipping, tumbling or shoved to the mat. Any combat gambit opens you up for countering. That's part of the game. But we have to ask ourselves if it is wise to choose gambits that allow for the possibility of countering ourselves.

This brings us to our next bias, utility, or ease of use. The theory of learning states that the less complex a skill set, the easier it is to be assimilated; conversely, the more complex the skill, the greater the time needed for assimilation. As this applies to our subject, low-kicks are rather easy to learn because they require minimum balance transfers and minimum flexibility. The speed required to launch a low-kick is minimal because we are traveling a short distance and firing from close range, thus making it less easily read by an opponent. These qualities make low-kicking attractive to the older athlete, the balance and flexibility impaired (you know who you are) and those with a low patience threshold.

By the way, there is nothing wrong with a low patience threshold. Our species wants maximum bang in minimum time, another point in favor of the low-kick dictum. We also know from stress studies that complex motor skills and high cognitive function are the first to go under duress (and a fight is indeed a stress situation). With this information in mind, we weight toward the low-kick as a simpler skill set to assimilate and more likely to survive a stress situation.

Speculation Corner
One of the hallmarks of martial arts dojo practice, demonstrations and fight cinema is high kicking, spinning kicks and kicks from all angles. Yet there is a dearth of them in MMA/NHB or security tapes, for that matter. One can't help but wonder why that is. It could be evidence of Darwinian technique selection as we see which techniques will and will not work in actual battlefield conditions, or it could be that stress inhibits the complex skill. I have no idea which of

these may be the correct answer. Perhaps it's a little of both or something completely different. But in light of this conspicuous absence, is there any real need to do all that work if the skill set disappears for whatever reason?

OK, if you're new to kicking and the low-kick-only dictum makes sense to you, you're in the right place. But what if you've already spent years perfecting a variety of high and spinning kicks? Does this mean you're wrong? Of course not. It means that if you can manage the balance transfers and skills of the high and spinning kicks, the low-kick arsenal found within will be a piece of cake. You should be able to assimilate the material at a rapid clip. You will have the benefit of launching the occasional high-kick when you see a prime opportunity. I beseech you not to fall prey to the "because it's there" fallacy of tool usage.

The "because it's there" trap is exhibited when a technique that may not be of absolute need is utilized simply because it's there. Think of all the camera phones today. Before the presence of these devices, I cannot recall meeting anyone who complained about needing a phone that also could take low-resolution photos of mundane things. Once the camera phone arrived on the scene, we witness countless individuals who deem the most prosaic of occasions as a "camera-phone moment." These same people likely own actual cameras that take high-quality photos, but they choose not to travel with them because they apparently never witnessed a moment worthy of documentation. Camera phone technology makes photo ops out of the quotidian.

High kicking often becomes "because it's there" technology. I keep a file of fights where one fighter has another in trouble (big trouble) and is putting the pressure on (as he should be) and then in the midst of using high-percentage finishers (hands), he steps back and decides to use the technology of the high-kick. What's the point of training it if you're not going to use it, right? This fight file documents many fights where the win was near, and then the break in pace to set up the "because it's there" tool allowed the opponent to cover, escape or retaliate. If you are going to use the high-kick because it's there, do yourself a favor and make sure it's *really* there.

Kicks must be placed in the proper perspective. Use the kick as one part of the whole — upper body striking tools, shooting, clinch work or submissions. Use them as setups, use them as punishers and use them as finishers if the opportunity presents. But do not fall prey to the "I use kicks to keep the opponent off me" silliness. This erroneous idea usually is rooted in the following substitute for reasoning: "Since the leg is the longest limb of the body, I can use the kick to keep an opponent from striking me with his hands or shooting in on me." Years of observation of MMA/NHB matches should have already put this idea to bed, but in case you haven't heard, please disregard this tactic.

Yes, the legs are the longest limbs on the body and can be placed between you and your opponent, but they can no more prevent an overwhelming onslaught than a bumper on a car prevents a collision. For those who fall back on the "legs are the artillery that keeps them away" rationale, keep in mind, artillery still needs support when the battle closes (and it does close, more often than not). Use the legs, learn to kick, but please place the tool in its correct context. There is no need to operate under fallacious strategies to have respect for the tool.

"OK, Mark. We get it — low-kicks are peachy, but do we really need an entire book devoted to the thigh kick? Isn't that overkill?" If you've already browsed through this book, you've seen that we have opened up the below-the-belt arsenal. We've increased the vocabulary beyond the standard thigh kick (an invaluable weapon) to include a variety of shots to the groin, to the inside and outside thighs, the shins, the patella, the biceps femoris tendons, the ankle, toes and instep. We use power shots, subtle shots, single shots, multiple shots and unique angles. We use out-range-to-in techniques, clinch kicking and level changes. We cover kicks to grounded opponents, we cover ... Just read on.

We don't cover knee attacks, that is using the knee as a weapon. Is that because we disregard the knee as an offensive tool? Nope. It's because we so value the knee as an offensive tool in all of its myriad applications that we will examine the knee in great depth in another volume. We have chosen to separate the low-kicks and the knees to show the proper deference to two formidable tool sets that should be part of all MMA/NHB/CQB fighters' arsenals.

TRAINING PROTOCOL

When working with the material in this book, I suggest the following template to guide you through the instruction in an orderly manner. It builds new skills upon previously learned ones. By approaching the subject in a synergistic-linear manner, you will find that the assimilation process is easier and you inoculate yourself against bad habits by starting at, well, the start.

Rounds over Repetitions

Not only do I suggest taking each portion of material as it comes, but also training with a round timer as opposed to merely counting repetitions. Counting repetitions engages the mind in a "keeping track" mode as opposed to an "evaluate performance" mode. You want to be evaluating your progress throughout.

I suggest setting the timer for 5-minute rounds to build endurance and to give you enough time to begin seating the given technique into your nervous system.

As each new aspect is introduced, I suggest working it for three 5-minute rounds to ensure comprehension. Once all the material has been introduced, you may walk through the book again from start to finish or hit sections of need or interest. Hit each piece of material in a single 5-minute round to touch up, hone or reemphasize a pet or needed tool.

Live Bodies over Target Tools
Kick shields are great. Thai pads are magnificent. Heavy bags are sublime. Training equipment has its place, but I highly suggest the use of live partner drilling from day one. Anyone who trains with us usually remarks on the fact that we gear up on day one and let the fun begin.

Don't misread that and assume that I am advocating whaling away on your partner with abandon. What I mean is: Put on the proper protective gear (for both receiving and delivering the arsenal tool in question), start the round timer and go to work delivering the technique in a 1-1 ratio.

1. You throw Technique A in a controlled manner against your partner.

2. Your partner returns.

3. And so on and so forth.

Use of live drilling from day one allows the fighter to visualize actual targets in motion, educate movement in real time, educate defense and offense simultaneously, and perhaps most important of all, hone the mental stance that is required to play a contact sport. No need to postpone the inevitable. Let's start the realistic feedback loop from the get-go.

Contact Again
The advocacy of launching against a live partner is not a license to injure, punish or humiliate. Use the 1-10 scale where a 1 is akin to a fraternal pat on the

back, and a 10 is competition full contact. Before you begin a drill, agree on a number, say 5. As the drill progresses, you may find that 5 is not enough, or too much, or that your definitions of 5 do not coincide. At this point, tell your partner to adjust the number up or down. By using the 1-10 scale you can stay in the arena of live drilling no matter the skill level you are playing with. In some cases, you may be launching 4's at your partner but receiving 8's. As long as you both are in agreement, it's all good.

Of course, there will come a point when you need to tee off and work the power shots. That's where your gear comes into play. Use the 5-minute rounds to learn the aliveness and begin to walk up the contact scale. When we see consistently good movement and technique at around a 7 on the scale, it is time to schedule some pure power work with equipment drills after live drilling.

Remember, live drilling is always emphasized over equipment drills.

Gear Usage
When it is time to use the gear, attempt to mimic live motion and human target positioning to the best of your ability. The Driller (pad holder/Coach) is just as important as the Drillee (striker). The Driller's job is to provide feedback (both verbal and contact bumps) to aid his partner. The Driller should be active, use footwork and the occasional evasion to make the Drillee stalk, retreat and so on. The Driller should hold gear as close to actual targets as safety permits. It is less than optimum to drill striking tools that are too far

away from the actual target (the human body). Remember, always let your training be reflective of the battlefield. When possible, emphasize live situations over simulations.

OK. With that preamble out of the way, let's get to work.

1 Stance

Your stance is a variation on the classic boxing guard with a bit wider positioning to allow for rapid defense and offense for shooting. Keep in mind that a stance is a reference point and not a stock-still animal. A stance blends and changes with movement, but you should always see the remnants of it even when in motion.

Stance

12-point stance

● Stand on the clock face with your lead foot at noon and your left foot at 8 if you are a right lead and your right foot at 4 if you are a left lead.

● Feet stay approximately a shoulder-width apart.

● Toes of both feet face slightly to the inside of your stance.

● Weight is felt on the balls of the feet without actually being tiptoed.

● Knees are slightly bent.

● Hands are up.

● Rear fist touches rear cheekbone.

● Lead fist at lead shoulder height extended approximately one foot in front of the shoulder.

● Elbows in.

● Forearms parallel.

● Chin down.

● Shoulders up.

No need to spend three 5-minute rounds on this, but you should assemble the stance in the mirror and watch for it devolving when approaching all of the material to follow.

2 Footwork

You can stand, now it's time to walk. Footwork is often overlooked by the novice because there is nothing dramatic about it. Veterans, on the other hand, are acutely aware that footwork/mobility often separates the Hitter from being the Hittee, the powerful effective strike from the just-missed shot.

Work each of the following footwork drills for the pre-scribed round protocol while watching for stance deterioration.

LAWS OF FOOTWORK

● Keep the feet one shoulder-width apart even while moving. Narrowing your base reduces balance and commensurately, reduces power.

● Resist the urge to hop or bounce with your steps. This showboating (some call it a needless waste of vital energy) inhibits speed, power and balance. In other words, a complete waste of your time and energy.

● The foot closest to your opponent is the lead foot. The one farthest is the trail foot. We violate this rule with stance shifting.

● Do not cross your feet when taking steps to move in any direction.

● Keep your feet in contact with the mat as much as possible even while stepping.

● Think step and drag, not step and step.

● Step in the direction you want to move with the foot nearest to that direction and then drag the trail foot to the new stance position, except in the case of stance shifting.

● Use a mirror to strive for footwork perfection.

● Once the mirror work is done, grab a partner and have them look for flaws while you move through several rounds of footwork.

● Keep your feet one shoulder-width apart when moving.

● Avoid bouncing, crossing your legs and high stepping.

THE GNOMON PRINCIPLE

The gnomon, for those who have started scratching their heads (I did the same thing the first time I encountered the word) is the upright stylus in the center of a sundial that is used to cast shadows to indicate approximate time. I want you to picture your-self as a gnomon standing on the surface of your sundial (your sundial being the mat, ring surface or street).

● When you stand in the center of your sundial, directly in front of you is 12.

● Behind you is 6.

● Directly to your right is 3 and to your left is 9.

● And so on with the numbers.

With the gnomon/sundial numbers in mind, let's begin our drills.

Step and drag forward

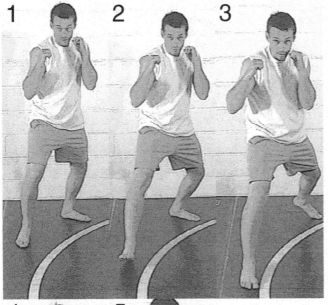

● Step the lead foot toward 12 and drag the trail foot to follow.

Step and drag retreat

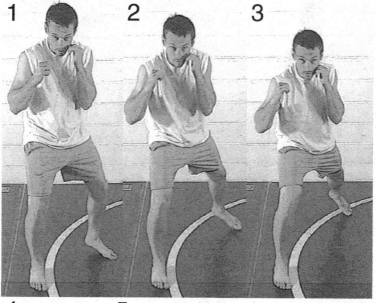

● Step the rear foot toward 6 and drag the trail foot to follow.

Step and outside drag

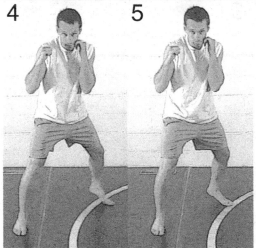

● Right side forward stancers will step to 3.
● Left leads will step to 9.

Step inside and drag

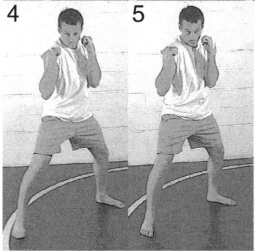

- Right leads will step to 9.
- Left leads to 3.

Stance shift

● The stance shift is exactly what it sounds like, a quick change in leads.

● Step the lead foot backward toward 6 leaving the left foot now closest to 12.

Step forward 45 degrees outside

● Right leads step the lead foot to 2.
● Left leads step the lead foot to 10.

Stance shift forward 45 degrees inside

● Right leads stance shift the left foot to 10.
● Left leads stance shift the right foot to 2.

Stance shift retreat 45 degrees outside

● Right leads stance shift the right foot to 5.
● Left leads stance shift the left foot to 7.

Stance retreat 45 degrees inside

- Right leads step to 7 with the rear foot.
- Left leads step to 5 with the rear foot.

Pivot inside

● A pivot is executed by leaving the lead foot in place and pivoting on the ball of that foot while the rear foot/trail foot sweeps in the prescribed direction.

● Right leads will sweep the rear foot to 10.

● Left leads will sweep the rear foot to 2.

Pivot outside

- Right leads will pivot the rear foot to 5.
- Left leads will pivot the rear foot to 7.

Once you have the basics of movement down, please do not think you have completed your footwork drills. On the contrary, you will be revisiting these time and time again. Optimally, you will learn each new kicking/striking tool in isolation (from a still stance). Then you will learn how to launch it effectively as you move forward, back, to the inside, outside and while pivoting. You must be able to fire while in motion, so know these numbers thoroughly. Then apply your striking tools on top of them.

These footwork drills will serve you in good stead as you develop or fine-tune your low kicking game. For advanced footwork options, upper body mobility and ring generalship concepts, please see our guide in this series, *Boxing Mastery*.

The Arsenal

It's time to start building the low kicking arsenal. We'll introduce each kick individually and then show how to apply them in multiples and combinations in later chapters. We begin with the outside range kicks. That is, kicks where there is no cohesion between you and your partner (cohesion defined as physical contact as in a clinch).

3 Outside range low-kick arsenal

REAR THIGH KICK

This is perhaps the hallmark of low kicking and with good reason. You will find this technique similar to the standard Muay Thai version, but with a little less commitment to avoid the spinning follow-through that is usually recommended. By abandoning the spin follow-through, we sacrifice a bit of power, but we make up for it in speed in combinations and the safety gained by not presenting the back. We are a bit lengthy with the initial explanations to seat fundamental technique. Later we pare down as we take these concepts for matter of fact.

● Right leads will step the lead foot to 2.

● Left leads will step to 10.

● Spinning on the ball of the lead foot, swing the rear leg from the floor to the target surface — the inside or outside of your opponent's thigh.

● The striking surface is the triangular facing surface of your shin (the tibia). Use the lower half of the tibia while being certain to use no lower portion of the leg. Striking with the ankle and/or the instep is a recipe for injuring yourself.

● You will recover the kick (negative motion or returning to stance) along the same path you throw the kick. Pay attention to negative speed (return speed). A quick return to position is what allows shifting into combinations and/or faster responses in defense work. Working only on striking speed with little attention paid to return speed is a common mistake.

• When throwing this kick, think of the leg as a club or tree limb that is being swung at your target. Do not hinge the leg and attempt to add more "snap" with a burst from the quadriceps upon contact. If it helps, think of the leg as one fused piece of bone with a slight bend in the knee so you aren't throwing stiff-legged.

• You also will find a bit more bite in the thigh-kick if you allow the kick to drop down upon impact.

• With that in mind, the complete arc described by the kick is the kick coming straight from the floor in a 45-degree and up angle and then a slight dip downward upon impact (exaggerated in the photo).

• This dip is executed by rolling the striking hip downward at the moment before impact.

• The hip is the key throughout this technique. You lead the kick from the hip allowing the leg to sweep along behind it. The more you concentrate on snapping the hip, and the less on swinging the leg, the more effective the kick.

Outside range low-kick arsenal

Rear thigh kick

Rear thigh kick / another view

Rear thigh kick / solo view

Rear kick ankle

● Here we have the exact same kick executed in an identical manner, but we change the target.

● The inner and outer surfaces of the ankle or lower shin are overlooked targets to bang. Strikes to the ankle have an unsettling caliber of pain and the added bonus of becoming leg sweeps/takedowns.

● The ankle as a target is also harder to read because the shot is faster, and they are seldom used (at the time of this writing). You should find that they are quite surprising to your opponent.

● Use them often.

Jumping rear kick thigh

● Uh-oh, I thought someone said no jumping kicks.

● This one is not a jumping kick in the usual sense.

● We use a shuffle step to close distance and strike when we've got an opponent drifting a bit too far on the periphery.

● The kick application is the same, once the shuffle step has been executed, so here we describe the shuffle/jump itself.

● Drive off your rear foot and take a lunging step toward the proper lead number (right leads to 2 and left leads to 10).

● As soon as the lead foot plants — launch the kick.

● We don't jump this kick to the ankle as the telegraphing of a hurtling body has a tendency to prompt a moved foot response. This usually still leaves the thigh as a target, but no need to chance the ankle from this outside range.

Switch kick thigh

● A switch kick is the mirror image of the rear kick thrown off the lead leg. But we perform a quick stance shift in front of it to load up the leg for greater power. That can be achieved by merely launching the lead leg straight from the floor.

● Right leads will skip the right leg toward 5 and the left leg toward 10.

● Left leads will skip the left leg toward 7 and the right leg toward 2.

● This stance shift skip happens simultaneously and with a ballistic burst of speed.

● From this new position, your "lead" leg has been positioned to the rear to deliver the standard "rear" thigh kick.

Switch kick ankle

● Switch as above and bang the ankle.

Switch kick / solo view

Slide switch kick thigh

● This is a less "acrobatic" version of loading up the switch kick.

● Right leads will drive off their rear foot and slide the lead foot toward 2.

● Left leads will drive with the rear foot to slide the lead foot to 10.

● Once you have stepped into the new number, step the rear foot forward (toward 12 for both leads).

Continued next page.

Slide switch kick thigh

- Now you launch a rear kick with your former lead leg.

- While not as fast as a standard switch kick, it still should be practiced with speed in mind. And you may be surprised how much speed you can muster in the midst of some footwork that can appear quite confusing to your opponent.

Slide switch kick thigh / solo

Inside kick thigh

● The inside kick is nothing more than a standard lead thigh kick delivered without the benefit of a hip windup, shuffle or slide-in assist.

● The kick is thrown off the lead leg and goes straight from the floor directly to its target.

● While there is no hip windup, it is advisable to aim for the hip roll-over upon the impact aspect of the technique.

● What the inside kick lacks in power, it makes up for in non-telegraphic speed.

Inside kick ankle

● Same kick, different target.

Shuffle-in inside kick thigh

● The shuffle-in allows you to use the inside kick even when your opponent is dancing in the outside range.

● To execute, both leads will slide the rear foot toward the lead (a bit of a footwork lawbreaking going on here, I know).

● Immediately drive off the rear leg to execute the inside kick with the lead leg.

● Work on the shuffle step until you gain the speed needed. Do not let the word "shuffle" lull you into being lackadaisical. Explode into technique whenever possible.

Shuffle-in inside kick ankle

● You know what to do.

Shuffle-in point round thigh

● In this version of the shuffle-in round, we make a few adjustments.

● First, the striking surface now is the ball of the foot (or the point of the shoe if shod).

● Second, we take advantage of the hinge nature of the knee joint.

● This is a variant of a kick found in Savate or La Boxe Francais with a bit less finesse.

● Shuffle-in as in the previous shuffle-in kicks.

● This time raise the lead knee high as if throwing a front kick to midsection level.

● Roll the hips so that the striking hip is pointing toward your target — the inner or outer thigh.

● Snap the kick using the quadriceps muscles to power the shot.

● While not a power shot by any stretch of the imagination, the small size and tenderness of the striking surface allows for an unsettling shot to be fired in the midst of combination work.

Shuffle-in point round groin

● Identical to the previous technique, but the target is the groin.

● This kick can be launched only if you are in matched leads (each of you has the right leg forward or each has the left forward).

Twist point thigh

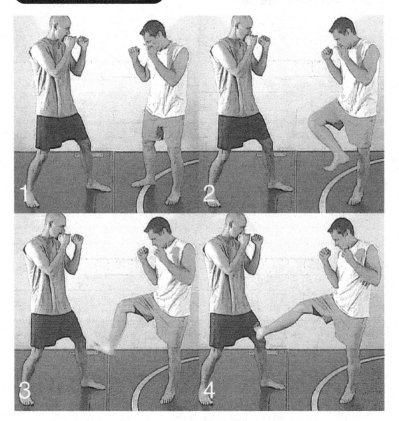

● This kick is an inverted version of the preceding two kicks.

● Twist points use an inverted action of the lead leg inside of the ankle up — an inversion of Savate technique.

● This kick (as with all of the point kick variants) is meant to be delivered with maximum snap/speed and minimum telegraphing.

Twist point groin

● Use twist point technique to strike the groin of an opponent standing in an unmatched lead.

Twist point / solo view

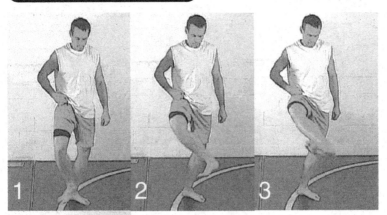

Lead bark

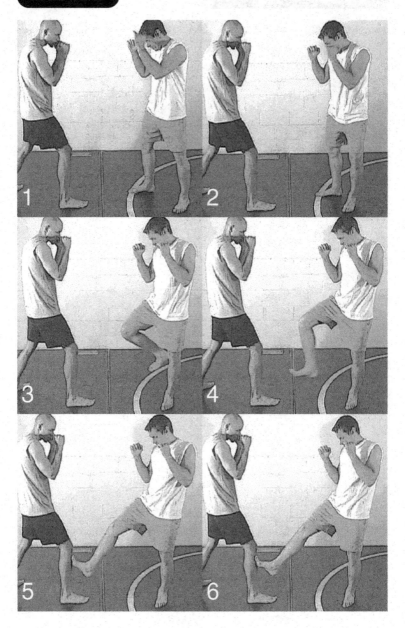

● Barks are best delivered with the point of the shoe and thus are ideal for self-defense and of little use for competition.

● Use the ball of the foot/point of the shoe of the lead leg to attack the shin or knee.

● Use the hinge action of the knee to deliver the kick.

● Strive for minimum telegraphing and maximum speed.

● The goal of the shoe and/or street oriented kicks is speed and strikes thrown in overwhelming numbers. No need to power up to throw these.

Rear bark

● The short choppy version thrown off the rear leg into the shin or knee.

Jab kick

● This kick is as high as we are going to throw in this manual.

● You will target your opponent's hips.

● It is used ideally as a range keeper (keeping your opponent away).

● Or as a stop kick to stop your opponent's attack.

● Or a distance creator, launching him back and away from you.

● Lift the lead knee high and then thrust the leg outward from this loaded position striking with either the ball of the foot or the entire sole of the foot.

● I urge you to target no higher than the hips for reasons offered in the introduction.

Shuffle-in jab kick

- Use standard shuffle-in technique and cock the lead knee high.

- Once the trail foot plants, launch the kick.

Descending jab kick

● This kick is a variant of the jab kick (as if the name didn't tip you off).

● Lift the knee high as in the standard jab kick, but rather than launch outward toward the hips, descend the sole of the foot on top of your opponent's thigh.

Stomp

- Here we fire a "jab" kick off the rear leg.
- It's a bit slower, but the power is greater.
- Lift the rear knee high.
- Deliver the kick striking with the ball of the foot. The target is your opponent's hips.
- Think of powering up to kick open a locked door and you've got the picture.

Cross stomp

● This also is delivered with the rear leg, but we strike with the entire sole of the foot. Toes are cocked to the outside and heel to the inside.

● This is a slightly more powerful variant of the preceding kick.

Stomps / solo views

Stomp above
and cross stomp
to the right.

Rear purring kick

● This self-defense kick is ideally delivered while wearing shoes.

● A purring kick is a cop from a Welsh drinking game in which participants clasped each other by the shoulders and took turns blasting each other in the shins with their hobnail boots. The first to release his shoulder grip lost.

● Here, the drinking is optional, we lose the shoulder clasp and simply deliver the kick.

● Travel the rear foot from the floor toward your opponent's lead shin. The toes point at the target.

● Just before contact, snap the toes to the outside and the heel to the inside.

● The striking surface is the inner arch of the foot.

Lead purring kick

● Since purring shots rely on speed over power, it is ideal to execute a short shuffle-in before delivering the kick like in the rear version.

Rear coup de pied bas

● This is a close relative of the purring kick found in Savate and La Boxe Francaise.

● The striking surfaces and targets are the same, but the foot travels along the floor until the energy release.

● Think of directing your striking heel toward the target, scuffing the foot along the floor and releasing this energy at the last moment to add to the snap.

Lead coup de pied bas

● Deliver as in the lead version, but provide a slight shuffle-in preceding the scuff-drag to provide greater snap/power.

Lead field goal

● Field goals are most defi-nitely self-defense kicks.

● Lift the lead knee and snap the lead shin (not foot) into your opponent's groin.

Rear field goal

● You think you can do some damage with the lead field goal — imagine what the rear field goal can do.

● Lift the rear knee and snap the shin into your opponent.

● For both versions of the field goal, think lifting your opponent off the planet. This will give you the idea of how they are intended to be delivered.

4 Clinch
low-kick arsenal

Kicks are usually thought of as outside tools, but they are mighty effective inside weapons as well. We will now explore some of the ways we can use kicks inside the clinch; whether that clinch be an over-under clinch, collar-and-elbow clinch, a biceps ride or a chaotic street encounter. All of the following kicks are based on the premise that there is some kind of cohesion with your opponent — you are gripping him, he is gripping you or you have a grip on each other. We do not instruct proper clinching technique here. You can find great detail in a previous manual in this series named *NHBF: The Clinch,* go figure. Many of these kicks are repeats of outside range kicks, but some are particular to this scenario.

Lead purring kick

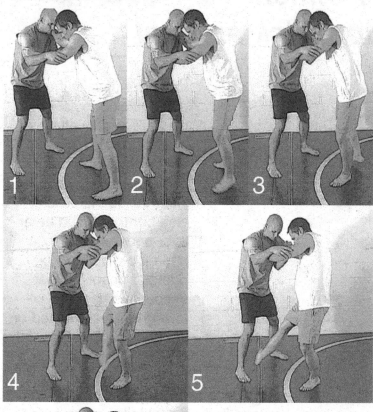

● Delivered in the same manner as the non-clinch version.

Rear purring kick

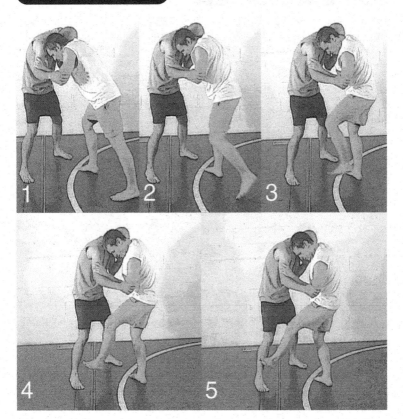

● You know what to do.

Lead coup de pied bas

● Ditto

Rear coup de pied bas

● Ditto

Clinch low-kick arsenal

Lead grater

● A grater is a self-defense shot meant to be delivered with the shoe.

● Think of it as a combination purring kick and foot stomp.

● To fire this one, launch a purring kick with the lead foot.

● Once the purring kick has struck the shin, rather than retract the kick, drive down his shin with the arch of your shoe in a cheese-grater fashion.

● At the bottom of this grating motion, deliver a foot stomp with the heel of the kicking foot.

● Although there are three distinct parts to this single technique, they are to be delivered in a continuous link with no obvious distinction among the parts.

Rear grater

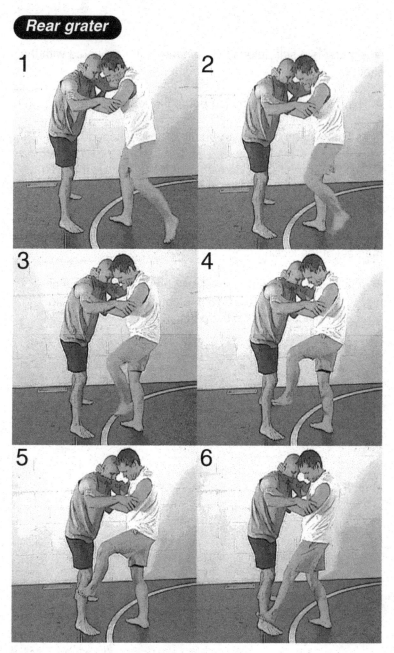

● Deliver this shot off the rear foot.

Lead bark

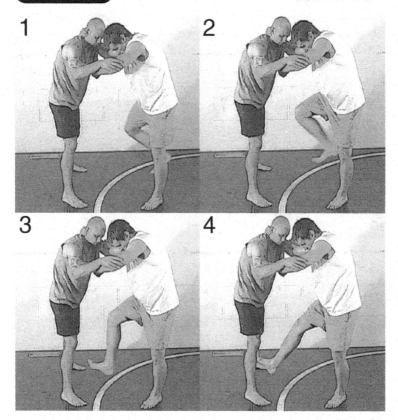

● The clinch version of the outside range bark. It is best delivered with the toe of the shoe.

Rear bark

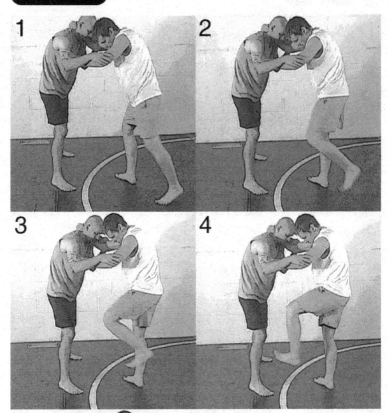

● Same kick; rear leg.

Rear inside crescent kick

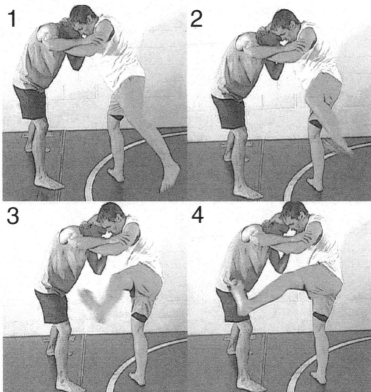

- Finally a pragmatic use for the traditional crescent kick.
- Strike with the inside of the shin.
- To deliver this kick, swing/snap the rear leg from the outside of your target (you can target the thigh or the shin).
- A short snap from the knee gives the kick the right amount of chop.

Lead inside crescent kick

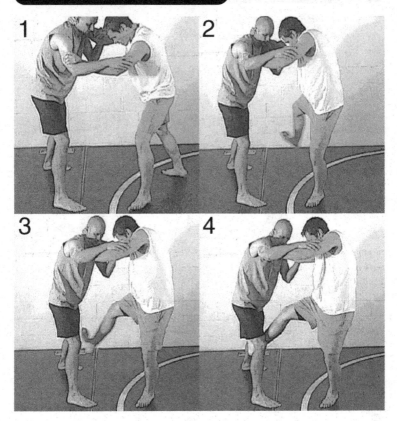

● Same kick launched off the lead leg.

Crescent kick / solo view

Toes-out foot stomp

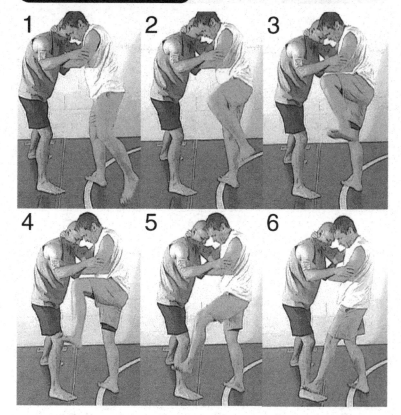

● Foot stomps are best delivered in a toes up, heel down position in order to strike with the hardest portion of the foot (the heel).

● You target the toes, instep and the often overlooked portion of the ankle where the shin and foot juncture.

● The toes-out version will be your most common version as you will (and should) be facing your opponent more often than not.

● Toes-out refers to the position of the foot — if you are striking his left foot with your right foot, the toes of the striking foot point toward the right.

● Work the foot stomps with both lead and rear legs.

Toes-in foot stomp

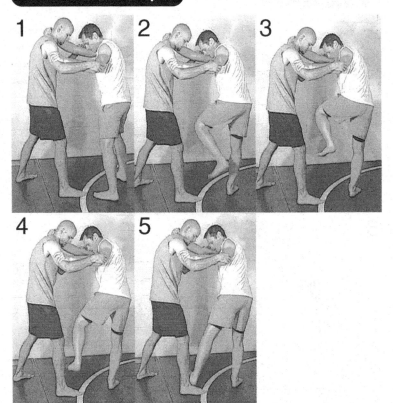

The striking surface remains the same, and the targets remain the same. What changes is the orientation of your foot upon delivery. You find yourself no longer in a nose on/squared off orientation with your opponent. Instead you find yourself with one side presented. You do not maneuver yourself to this position, but find yourself outclassed to this spot.

● Strike and get back to square.

● Work both the lead and rear foot versions.

Foot trapping

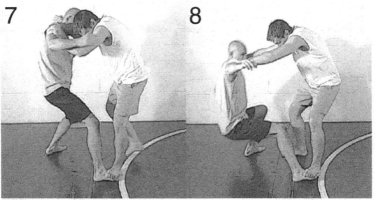

● Foot trapping can follow the graters or either version of the foot stomps.

● At the end of the foot stomp, leave your weight on your opponent's foot rather than retracting your foot.

● With his foot in this "trapped" position — shove him.

● Best case scenario is a broken foot.

● At least you will break his balance and send him to the mat.

Step right up

● This technique is nothing more than foot trapping as described above, but used when you have a body lock out of your clinch (described in detail in our book, *NHBF: The Clinch*).

● Once you have the foot trapped, lift with your body lock putting a bit of hyperextension pressure on your opponent's ankle.

● Admittedly this move is for heavy weight classes and more iffy than the other shots, so consider your strength options before giving it too much focus.

Heel chops

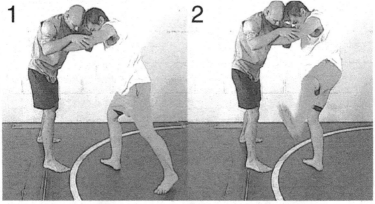

● This is a very nasty kick that should be a major part of your clinch kick arsenal.

● You can deliver this shot with either the lead or rear leg (by all means practice them both).

● The striking surface is the back of the heel, and the target is the outside tendon of your opponent's knee.

● To deliver, lift the kicking knee to waist level with the striking heel to the outside of his knee.

● Use the hamstring muscles of the kicking leg to snap the heel (in a scooping manner) into the target.

5 Cut kicking

Muay Thai has made an art and science out of cut kicking, and we would be remiss not to include the concept in our low kicking agenda. I warn you, cut kicking is timing dependent, meaning you must have good perceptual speed/technique reading ability to make this tactic successful. The cut kick tactic is best utilized against a high kicking opponent. If you are both staying in the realm of low kicking then you may never find yourself presented with cut kicking opportunities. So with those odds in mind, determine for yourself how much time you wish to devote to the topic.

With that out of the way, let's define cut kicking for the uninitiated. To cut kick is to deliver a stop kick beneath your opponent's higher level kick thus "cutting" his support leg out from under him. Keep in mind the cut kick ideally is used against an opponent's rear leg kicks because the additional distance he travels assists in technique reading.

Matched lead cut kick

● When your matched lead opponent throws his high rear kick, you fire a quick inside kick to his supporting leg.

● You should have more of a backward lean than usual from your upper body so you can remove his target (your head).

Unmatched lead cut kick

● Against the unmatched lead, fire your own rear kick to the supporting leg versus the high rear kick of your opponent.

● The same rearward lean and paying attention to guard considerations are in play.

Matched lead side kick

● If the prospect of building the timing to deliver a cut kick versus a matched lead seems a bit daunting, you can try this simpler variant.

● Fire the lead leg side kick as your cut kick while paying attention to the rearward lean and guard.

6 Rear clinch kicks

These are self-defense kicks or kicks to be used (rules permitting) when your opponent has you in a rear clinch. As a rule never sacrifice your base/balance to throw one of these kicks. The fact that your opponent has been able to take your back already tells you something about his skill. Bend at the waist, guard your base and then consider whether or not you can throw one of these kicks safely.

Rear clinch kicks

Toes-out foot stomp

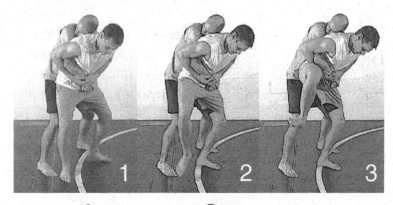

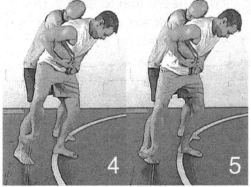

● Deliver the standard toes-out foot stomp from the rear clinch position.

● This is delivered off either foot.

Donkey kick shin / knee

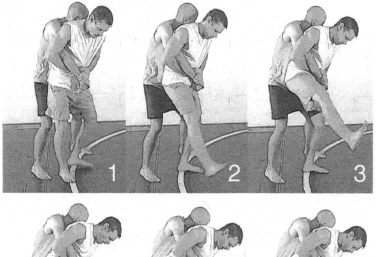

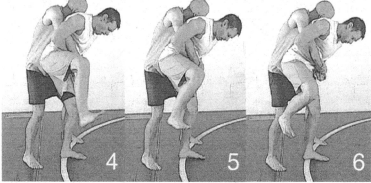

● This shot also can be thrown off either leg.

● Lift the kicking knee and leave a 90-degree angle bend in your leg.

● Chop the heel backward catching him in either the shin or knee.

Heel scoop groin

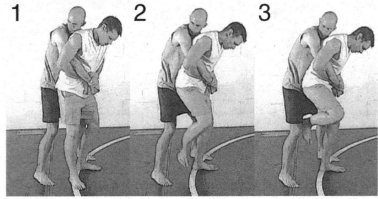

● Again, this one can be delivered with either leg.

● It is similar to the preceding, but the angle of delivery changes.

● In this kick, the kicking heel scoops back and up to target the groin.

7 Kick combinations

It's time to start firing kicks in multiples. Here are a few thoughts to keep in mind.

1. We address kick-only combinations; we'll discuss integration with upper body tools next.

2. Kicking combinations flow less naturally than hand combinations, so we'll keep the combination numbers low.

3. Not all the possible combinations nor all the arsenal kicks are demonstrated or utilized. These combinations are meant to serve as examples to educate the legs to fire fast and often.

4. We weight the material toward the round kicks since they are the most common in MMA and street work.

KICKING COMBINATIONS

- DOUBLE REAR KICK THIGH
- DOUBLE SWITCH KICK THIGH
- DOUBLE REAR KICK ANKLE
- DOUBLE SWITCH KICK ANKLE

- DOUBLE REAR KICK ANKLE / THIGH
- DOUBLE SWITCH KICK ANKLE / THIGH
- DOUBLE REAR KICK THIGH / ANKLE
- DOUBLE SWITCH KICK THIGH / ANKLE

- REAR KICK THIGH / SWITCH KICK THIGH
- SWITCH KICK THIGH / REAR KICK THIGH
- REAR KICK ANKLE / SWITCH KICK ANKLE
- SWITCH KICK ANKLE / REAR ANKLE

- REAR KICK THIGH / SWITCH KICK ANKLE
- SWITCH KICK THIGH / REAR KICK ANKLE
- REAR KICK ANKLE / SWITCH KICK THIGH
- SWITCH KICK ANKLE / REAR KICK THIGH

- DOUBLE REAR KICK THIGH /
  DOUBLE SWITCH KICK THIGH
- DOUBLE REAR KICK ANKLE /
  DOUBLE SWITCH KICK ANKLE
- DOUBLE REAR KICK THIGH / ANKLE /
  DOUBLE SWITCH KICK THIGH / ANKLE
- DOUBLE REAR KICK ANKLE / THIGH
  DOUBLE SWITCH KICK ANKLE / THIGH

● LEAD BARK / REAR BARK
● REAR BARK / LEAD BARK

● LEAD PURR / REAR PURR
● REAR PURR / LEAD PURR

● LEAD BARK / REAR PURR
● INSIDE KICK / REAR PURR
● SWITCH KICK THIGH / REAR PURR
● SWITCH KICK ANKLE / REAR PURR

● INSIDE KICK / LEAD SIDE TO FAR KNEE
  (One movement without putting the kicking leg down).
● SHUFFLE INSIDE KICK / REAR KICK THIGH /
  LEAD FIELD GOAL
● DOUBLE INSIDE KICK / REAR KICK THIGH

8 Kicking with upper body combinations

Here, we provide a good template to integrate your upper body tools with the low-kick material. For more information on the upper body arsenal, see our books *NHBF: Savage Strikes* and *Boxing Mastery*.

Kicking with upper body combinations

● JAB / REAR KICK

● CROSS / SWITCH KICK

Kicking with upper body combinations

● JAB KICK / CROSS

● JAB / CROSS / HOOK / REAR KICK

● REAR KICK / CROSS / LEAD HOOK

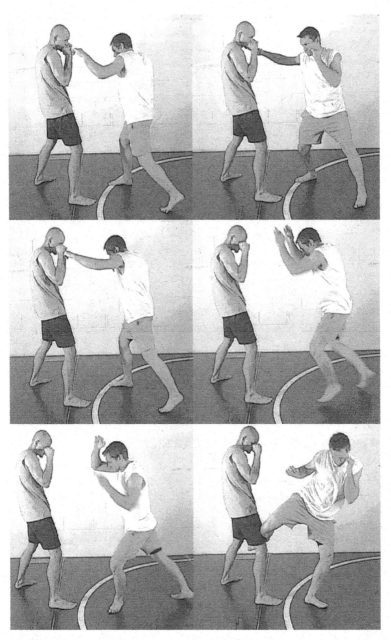

● CROSS / HOOK / CROSS / SWITCH KICK

● HOOK / CROSS / HOOK / REAR KICK

● JAB KICK / CROSS / HOOK / CROSS

Kicking with upper body combinations

● JAB / INSIDE KICK / CROSS / REAR KICK

● REAR STOMP / HOOK / CROSS / SWITCH KICK

● DOUBLE JAB / CROSS / UPPERCUT / CROSS / SWITCH KICK

9 The ax murderer series

It's time to address kicking a downed opponent. This section, of course, is named for the great fighter Vanderlai Silva who raised this sort of attack to a level of brutal efficiency.

POSITION STRIKES

We begin by addressing kicks to a downed opponent in the quarter position, turtle position, or more simply, on his hands and knees.

SOCCER KICK

● The soccer kick is a line drive, boot-the-ball-down-the-field kick delivered with either the rear or the lead foot in a switch kick/stance shift fashion.

● Strive to use the shin as the striking surface.

● You can fire the soccer kick to whatever targets your rules allow.

Soccer kick to head

Soccer kick to brachial plexus

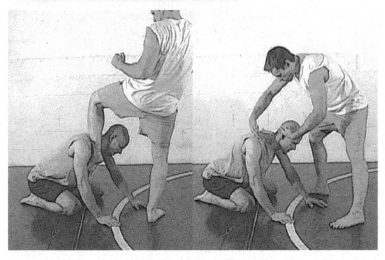

● To avoid the painful prospect of breaking your foot on your opponent's head, target the soft tissue found in the "L" of the side of the neck and top of the shoulder.

Soccer kick to ribs

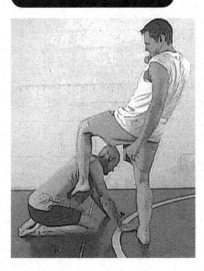

● When striking the ribs, it is always more damaging to aim low on the rib cage. This increases the odds of catching floating ribs as opposed to the more solid structure found closer to the armpit.

STOMPS

● Just as with the foot stomp, you strike with the heel.

● Practically all targets on the body are choice. The following two suggestions are often overlooked although exceptionally damaging.

Stomp to achilles tendon

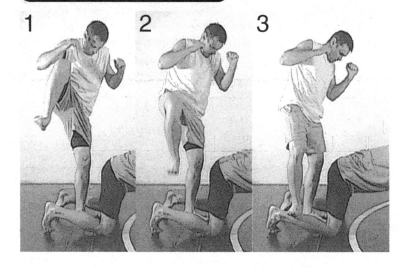

Stomp to hands

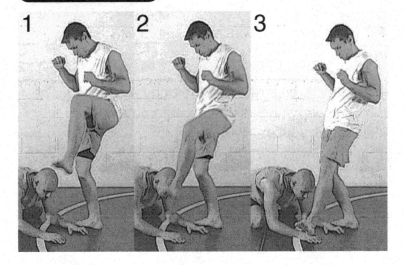

KICKING A GROUNDED OPPONENT

We classify an opponent who is lying down, either supine or prone, as a grounded opponent. There are a few choice strategies for the grounded fighter (the one on the ground) that we'll cover at a later date. Here, we'll address attacks on the grounded opponent.

Soccer kick head

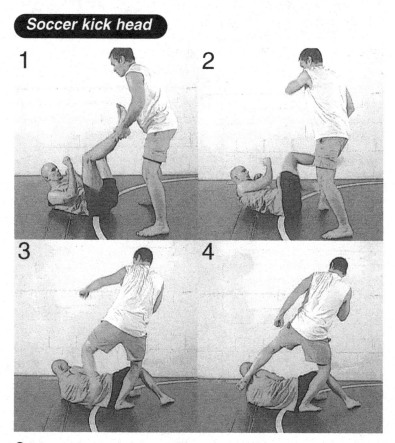

● It is tough not to strike with the ankle or instep, so strike with caution.

The ax murderer series

Stomp head

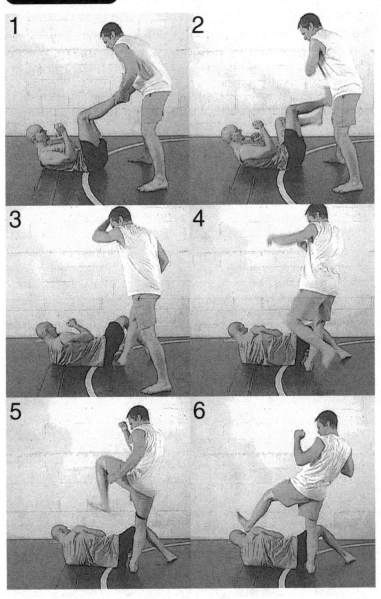

Stomp body

Stomp feet

1 2

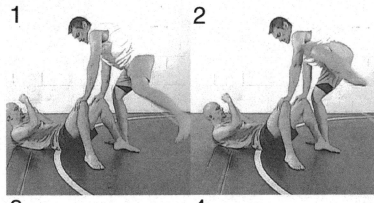

3 4

5

Flying stomp

● Not recommended because of the chances of being speared in the groin (last image), but it is fun.

SPRAWL AND KICK DRILL

● We group this drill with the ground kicking material because it allows for kicking in transition on the ground (or attempted transition).

To perform this drill, grab a partner and hit the timer.

● Your partner shoots a takedown.

● Post and sprawl.

● Pop up immediately and soccer kick.

● For detailed information on either takedowns or takedown defense, see our book in this series, *NHBF: Takedowns.*

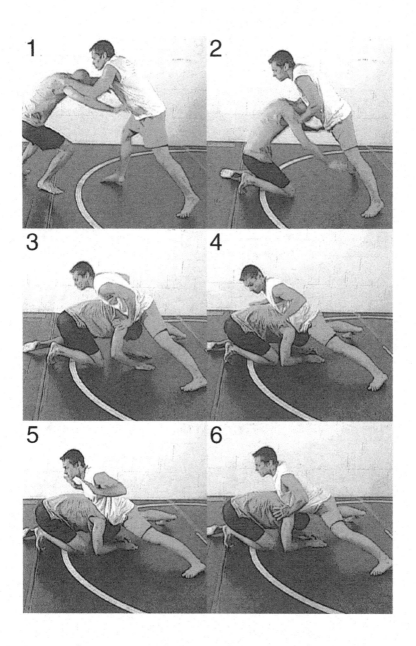

Sequence continues next page

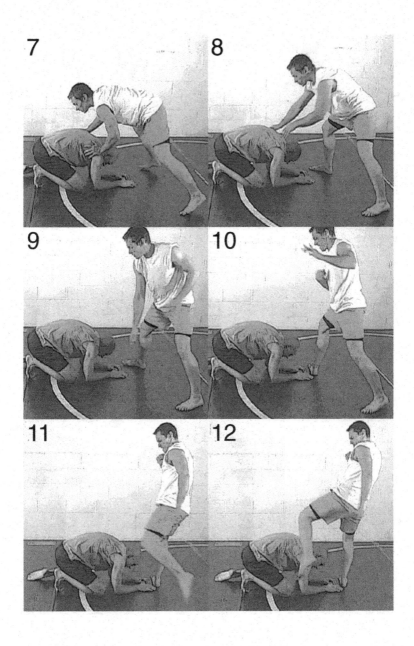

Kick Defense

That completes the low-kick arsenal. Now it's time to educate the converse — defense. Although we advocate kicking at the low angle, we cover defenses for high and mid-level kicks since you will more than likely encounter them.

Although defense isn't quite as dramatic to work as offense, please observe the same round protocol to best learn the material.

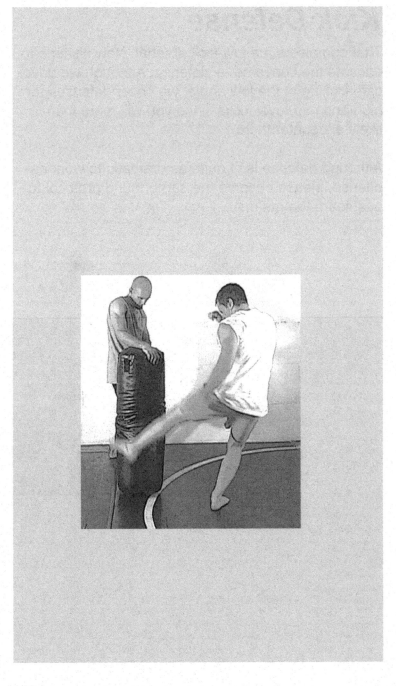

10 Low round kick defenses

KNEE CHECK

● We recommend directing the point of the knee into the oncoming kick as opposed to shin blocking. Your opponent will find the knee point far more disconcerting than you. Gear up and train with caution.

● There is no need to "strike" with the knee point because the damage is done by your opponent kicking into your knee point.

● Lift and point the knee versus a kick from the mirror side. This means if he kicks with his right leg, you knee check with your left leg.

● On all knee checks, pull the heel back toward your butt to create a quasi-ramp. This ramp construction is a built-in safety precaution. If you misjudge your knee point, the ramping diffuses kick power as it travels down the shin using the standard leg check form as a fallback.

Cross knee check

● Lift and point the same side knee, right versus right.

Low round kick defenses

● Drive off your lead foot and retreat — taking yourself out of range.

Stance shift

● Stance shift rearward to change range.

Foot jab stop kick to body

● You can use a quick foot jab to the low round kicker's hips to stop the kick and blow him off base.

Foot jab stop kick to attacking leg

● Apply the same idea to the kicking leg. It's easier than you might imagine with a little practice. A straight line beats an angle every day of the week. This defense is akin to using the jab to stop hit a hook in boxing.

11 High and medium round defenses

High round stonewall

● Against a head kick, execute the same stonewall as you would for a high hook punch.

● To stonewall, fold your arm over your ear, elbow down.

● As the kick makes contact, strive to lean toward the opponent to cut a bit off the power angle.

● It is optimum to take the kick with both folded halves of the arm (upper and lower arm) as opposed to just one portion of the arm.

Medium round stonewall

● Against body kicks, you execute the same stonewall defense as for high round kicks. But the stonewall is at a lower level.

● Remember to use both gates of the arm and not merely your forearm.

12 Low straight kick defenses

Knee point

● The knee point won't damage your opponent in this case, but it removes your knee from jeopardy.

Step back

● You know what to do.

13 Medium straight kick defenses

Stonewall

● Here your opponent fires a straight kick at your body.

● Close the forearm shells and sink your hips back upon impact to mitigate the blow.

Hip fade

● Shift your hips rearward to move or fade the target away from your opponent.

Knee check / solo view

● You can use the knee check in a quasi-inside crescent kick fashion to redirect mid-level straight kicks.

● Here we use the lead knee.

Medium straight kick defenses

Knee check

Step back

● You know what to do.

Stance shift

● Ditto.

Step back and scoop vs jab kicks

● Step back.

● Underhook the kicking ankle with the lead hand and lift.

Pivot and scoop vs jab kicks

- Pivot to the inside.

- Underhook his kicking heel with your lead hand.

- Toss his leg to his inside.

Scoop and cut

● Scoop with the lead hand and then return a cut kick.

14 High straight and purring kick defenses

Stonewall

● Against a high straight kick to your head, close the parallel shells of your forearms to deflect the attack.

● Give a slight rock back with the body for shock absorbance.

Purring point

● The knee point also can be used to counter purring kicks.

● Point the tip of your knee high on your opponent's shin to take a lot of the steam out of his purring attack.

Lift

● It is a fact that merely lifting the leg should steer you clear of the vast majority low kick/stomp offenses.

15 Pick offs

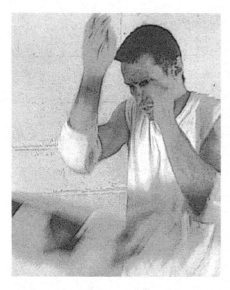

Pick offs are an aggressive form of defense that we've already seen demonstrated in the form of the knee point. The idea is to alter slightly the target the opponent is seeking so that it provides a self-inflicting injury on the offender. Pick offs are not fight enders in and of themselves, but they go a long way toward making your opponent's offense hesitant and/or more languid than he planned.

Although it is attractive to start with pick offs since they have a little bite to them, please learn standard defense first. Then add the pick off concept to your game.

High round kick pick off

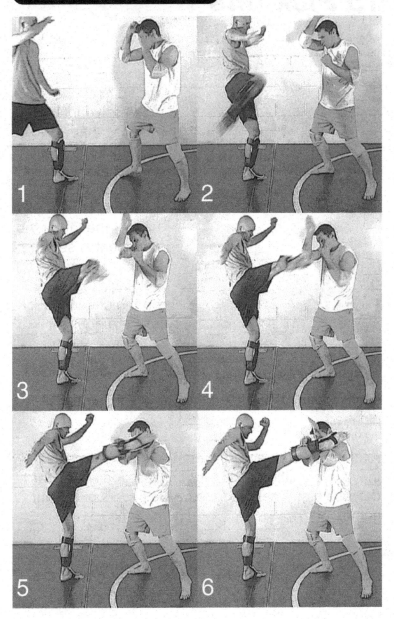

● You still use the stonewall strategy, but with a small adjustment.

● You use one hand to guide the incoming head kick to your other elbow.

● To execute this technique:

1. Lead hand guide to rear elbow.

2. Rear hand guide to lead elbow.

Mid round kick pick off

● Here you use the exact same strategy, techniques and limb combinations as in the high round pick offs.

A closer view

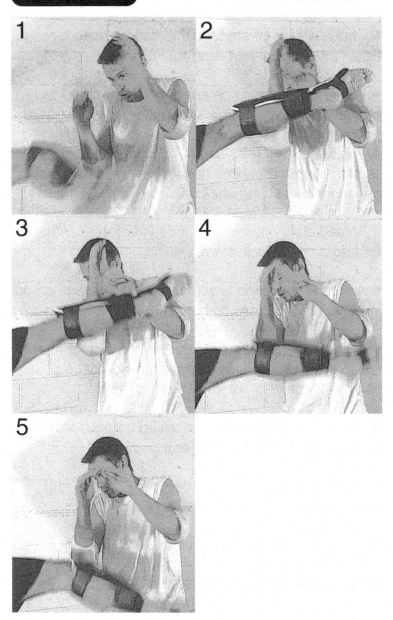

KNEE DRAG

● This is a pick off strategy that can be used for either the high- or mid-level round kicks.

● I suggest you become adept at the standard pick offs before moving to the knee drags.

● The knee drag is executed by using the twin shields of your forearms (inner forearms facing your opponent's incoming shin).

● Immediately upon impact, use your forearms/hands to drag/slap the kick down.

● As the kicking limb is slapped down, execute an up knee into the slapped limb.

● The knee is always executed on the side of attack. Example: A kick delivered to the left side of your body will receive a left knee and vice versa.

● The knee drag can be performed on each side of the body and for both head and body kicks.

● It also can be used in tandem with the previous kick pick offs.

1. Lead hand guide to rear elbow to knee drag.

2. Rear hand guide to lead elbow to knee drag.

A closer view

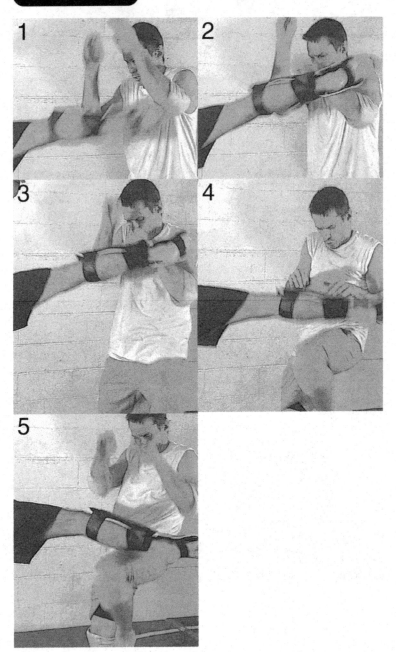

TOE KICK

● Against all high kicks, you always have the option of firing a lead snap front kick into the groin of the high kicker.

● Use the toes as the striking surface (when wearing shoes the damage is even greater). Catching an opponent's groin in this "stretched" position is quite, um, disconcerting.

Remember, pick offs are meant to be added to your defensive tools, not to be used in place of them. Be sure that your stonewall is firm and reflexive before adding the pick off extras. Each tool in your defensive arsenal should be drilled in isolation rounds and then in combination to ensure fluidity of movement.

16 Kicking chain drills

Just as we build offensive/defensive/counteroffensive chain drills with our boxing and grappling material, we want to build one with kicking integrated with other tools. We don't have the space to present combinations into the stratosphere, but you will find the following drills enough to understand the template to build your own drills.

In each of the following drills, the movement inside parentheses is what the Feeder/Driller/Coach performs. I suggest approaching the drills following this gradient.

1. Perform a single 5-minute round of each individual link in the chain as it comes. For example, take the first drill. Do one round with your Coach firing the inside kick while you stance shift.

2. Next round, you stance shift versus the inside kick and return the rear kick.

3. Next you play the role of Coach/Driller/Feeder and fire the inside kick while he stance shifts and so on and so on.

4. Approach each drill in this manner even if it has numerous steps. Reversing the roles allows you to grasp the material more easily.

- (INSIDE KICK) STANCE SHIFT / REAR KICK

- (REAR KICK) STANCE SHIFT / REAR KICK

- (JAB KICK) FADE / REAR KICK

- (JAB KICK) STEP BACK AND SCOOP / REAR KICK

- (JAB KICK) PIVOT AND SCOOP / REAR KICK

- (JAB KICK) KNEE CHECK / REAR KICK

- (ROUND KICK) KNEE POINT / REAR KICK
  OR SWITCH KICK

- JAB / CROSS (JAB KICK) SCOOP / REAR KICK

- (JAB) SLIP / CROSS / HOOK / CROSS / SWITCH KICK

- (JAB) CATCH / JAB / CROSS / HOOK / REAR KICK

- (HOOK) COVER / HOOK / CROSS / HOOK / SWITCH KICK

Again, this is only a handful of ideas in an area that deserves a great deal of attention. Do yourself a favor and learn these drills inside out and then concoct your own. At the high end of striking training, you should spend the vast majority of your time on intensive chain drilling.

17 Kicking conditioning drills

The following drills are specific to building conditioning/fitness for powerful kicking. There are, of course, many permutations of these drills, and I encourage you to experiment. For further ideas on conditioning specific to NHB/MMA and street defense, see our volume in this series, *NHBF: The Ultimate Guide to Conditioning.*

First, a note on our preference for floor bags. We use heavy bags stood on end as opposed to hanging for these reasons:

1. A hanging bag invites kicking higher than we advocate simply because the target is there.

2. The upright floor bag provides a great amount of friction on the mat. This "no give" goes a long way toward building power.

3. A floor bag must be supported by a Coach/partner. This invites constant feedback, which is always a good thing.

4. The floor bag invites quick transition between upright floor bag work and ground floor bag work. This fluid transition between drill sets is invaluable in learning to blend ranges as opposed to cross-training ranges.

8-COUNT
KICK SQUATS

1. SQUAT
2. RIGHT FRONT KICK

3. SQUAT
4. LEFT FRONT KICK

5. SQUAT
6. RIGHT ROUND KICK

7. SQUAT
8. LEFT ROUND KICK

COUNTDOWNS

- Use a floor bag or kick shield.
- Start with a single rear kick or switch kick.
- Climb to 10 repetitions and then back down.
- Repeat with the opposite leg.

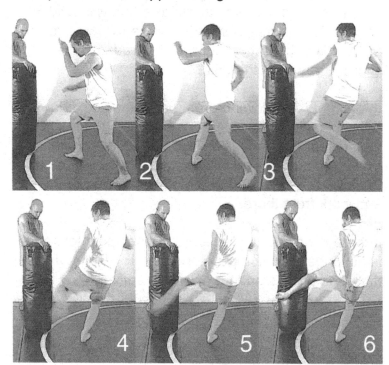

BAG WALKS

- Have your partner support a floor bag on its end.
- Use the rear kick to move it along the floor the entire length of the gym.
- Use the opposite leg to bring it back.

LEG CONDITIONING DRILLS

I don't recommend isolated drills for pain tolerance. No need for kicking trees and the like. That sort of training is the stuff of cinema and legends. You should find that by working the bag and partner drills, a certain degree of pain acclimatization will build. If you still find yourself gun-shy, try the following drills. Demanding that the partners clinch reduces the ability to run from the drill.

In each of the following drills, use the elbow ride: palm C hand in your partner's biceps. The idea is to maintain partner cohesion and trade blows in a tit-for-tat manner as you walk up the 1-10 scale. Once the level has been found, drop back down a number and work from there.

If there is no gun-shy attribute or once pain tolerance is no longer a major issue, feel free to discard these drills and allow standard drilling to suffice.

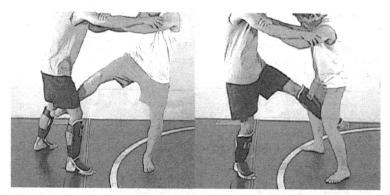

ELBOW RIDE INNER THIGH KICKS

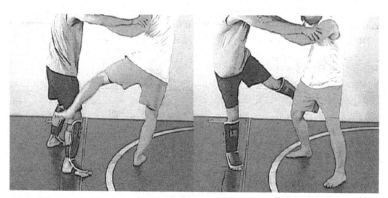

ELBOW RIDE OUTER THIGH KICKS

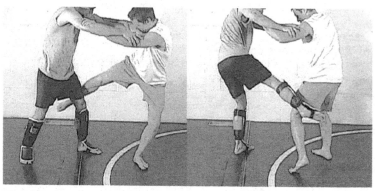

ELBOW RIDE SHIN CRESCENT THIGH KICKS

Resources

BEST CHOICES

First, please visit my Web site at
www.extremeselfprotection.com
You will find even more training
material as well as updates and
other resources.

Amazon.com

The place to browse for books such
as this one and other similar titles.

Paladin Press
www.paladin-press.com

Paladin carries many training
resources as well as some of my
videos, which allow you to see
much of what is covered in my
NHB books.

Ringside Boxing
www.ringside.com

Best choice for primo equipment.

Sherdog.com

Best resource for MMA news, event
results and NHB happenings.

Threat Response Solutions
www.trsdirect.com

They also offer many training
resources along with some of my
products.

Tracks Publishing
www.startupsports.com

They publish all the books in the
NHBF series as well as a few fine
boxing titles.

www.humankinetics.com

Training and conditioning info.

www.matsmatsmats.com

Best resource for quality mats at
good prices.

Video instruction

Extreme Self-Protection
extremeselfprotection.com

Paladin Press
paladin-press.com

Threat Response Solutions
trsdirect.com

World Martial Arts
groundfighter.com

Events

IFC
ifc-usa.com

IVC
valetudo.com

King of the Cage
kingofthecage.com

Pancrase
so-net.ne.jp/pancrase

Pride
pridefc.com

The Ultimate Fighting
Championships
ufc.tv

Universal Combat Challenge
ucczone.ca/

Index

Boxing Mastery
Advance Techniques, Tactics and
Strategies from the Sweet Science
1-884654-21-5 / $12.95
Advanced boxing skills and ring general-
ship. 900 photos.

No Holds Barred Fighting:
Takedowns
Throws, Trips, Drops and Slams for NHB
Competition and Street Defense
1-884654-25-8 / $12.95
850 photos.

No Holds Barred Fighting:
The Clinch
Offensive and Defensive Concepts
Inside NHB's Most Grueling Position
1-884654-27-4 / $12.95
750 photos.

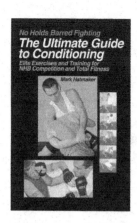

No Holds Barred Fighting:
The Ultimate Guide to Conditioning
Elite Exercises and Training for NHB
Competition and Total Fitness
1-884654-29-0 / $12.95
192 pages / 900 photos

Videos by Mark Hatmaker available through Paladin

THE ABCs OF NHB
High-Speed Training for No-Holds-Barred Fighting

BEYOND BRAZILIAN JUJITSU
Redefining the State of the Art in Combat Grappling

EXTREME BOXING
Hardcore Boxing for Self-Defense

THE FLOOR BAG WORKOUT
The Ultimate Solo Training for Grapplers and Groundfighters

GLADIATOR CONDITIONING
Fitness for the Modern Warrior (with companion workbook)

THE SUBMISSION ENCYCLOPEDIA
The Ultimate Guide to the Techniques and Tactics of Submission
Fighting

THE COMPLETE GRAPPLER
The Definitive Guide to Fighting and Winning on the Ground
(with companion workbook)

Paladin Enterprises, Inc.
7077 Winchester Circle
Boulder, CO 80301 USA
303.443.7250 303.442.8741 fax
www.paladin-press.com

Mark Hatmaker is the author of all seven books in the bestselling *No Holds Barred Fighting Series* and *Boxing Mastery*. He also has produced more than 40 instructional videos. His resume includes extensive experience in the combat arts including boxing, wrestling, Jiujitsu and Muay Thai.

He is a highly regarded coach of professional and amateur fighters, law enforcement officials and security personnel. Hatmaker founded Extreme Self Protection (ESP), a research body that compiles, analyzes and teaches the most effective Western combat methods known. ESP holds numerous seminars throughout the country each year including the prestigious Karate College/Martial Arts Universities in Radford, Virginia. He lives in Knoxville, Tennessee.